The Lightbringers

Karin Celestine

This book belongs to

For Hudson

with love

Karin Celestine

Huge gratitude to Tamsin Rosewell for the drawings,
Cecilia Hewett for proofreading and
Pamela Thom-Rowe for the folklore information.

The Lightbringers published by Graffeg in 2020.
Copyright © Graffeg Limited 2020.

Text and photographs copyright © Karin Celestine,
illustrations copyright © Tamsin Rosewell, design and production Graffeg
Limited. This publication and content is protected by copyright © 2020.

Karin Celestine is hereby identified as the author of this work in accordance with
section 77 of the Copyrights, Designs and Patents Act 1988.

A CIP Catalogue record for this book is available from the British Library.

ISBN 9781913634193

1 2 3 4 5 6 7 8 9

For more of the world of Celestine and the Hare
visit www.celestineandthehare.com.

The Lightbringers

Karin Celestine

For all who walk with a quiet heart but especially
for Jennie, a warrior of the light.

GRAFFEG

The Earth breathes.

In the summer, she breathes out and the world fills with warmth and light. She laughs and dances and the flowers spill out from her cloak.

Folk feast on the fruits of summer and make flower crowns. They dance and light bonfires, jumping them for courage.

When the Earth has danced and laughed till she is tired, she settles down to sleep. The flowers gather up the light and warmth and hold it in their fruits and seeds. They glow with the warmth of her dancing.

Autumn comes and folk gather in the harvest, saying thanks for the gifts of summer. They bake harvest loaves and make ready for the cold to come.

Small creatures hide the light away in their burrows and dens.

The Earth breathes in.

She breathes in the light for warmth as she sleeps.

The creatures keep safe the last sparks of light deep underground.

She slumbers and dreams of summer and flowers and dancing. While she dreams, her cloak gets cold and flowers of ice crystals grow. Their beauty reminds folk of the summer flowers, but the colour and warmth have gone.

She breathes in further and it becomes dark.

We feel like the light will never come back again.

The Small Ones burrow down, guarding the light.

She breathes in further and dreams her dreams.

The cold bites and the darkness enfolds.

But then, she shifts in her slumber.

There is a pause.

The pause between breath in and out,
between heart beats.

The still dark turning point.

The solstice.

The turn.

The turn of the year.

Folk bring in trees and decorate their hearths.

They light candles and yule logs to remind them of the warmth and light they long for.

The creatures feel the pause and the shift and murmurings of Earth's sleep.

And so it begins.

At the sound of her out breath, the Hare, who has guarded the moon full of the silver shining light of the sun, calls the Small Ones to her.

All through the darkness, small beings gather up the tiny sparks, almost extinguished, but not quite.

They take the embers and gently place them in their seed lanterns and they start to walk.

One by one, they come out and gather together.

The Lightbringers.

The Bearers of Spring.

They find each other in the darkness and they walk. They scurry through hedges and woodlands.

They pass the Mari Lwyd, the riddle horse, on her procession through towns and villages.

They pass the Wassailers, the tree guardians, singing loud songs and banging their pots and pans in the orchards.

Most don't notice the Lightbringers, but those who are quiet of heart, who walk the hedges and honour the Earth, might catch a glimpse.

As the Earth turns in her sleeping, she breathes out. The long, slow breath that will warm her and bring the flowers and her laughter.

As she turns, as she breathes, the Hare keeps calling and they come. In ones and twos, in small groups, they walk and gather.

The Earth breathes out and the Lightbringers find each other as they follow the call of the Hare to Spring.

Onward they keep walking. When they start to tire
and falter, the Badger appears to call them on,
to remind them they are not alone, that others too
are walking with the light.

And soon they are gathered in enough numbers
that folk start to notice the light returning.
The birds start to sing a little earlier.
The Earth starts to warm as she breathes out.

The Lightbringers combine their tiny sparks to light the Earth once more and she starts to wake.

She smiles at the warmth and dreams of dancing flowers.

She smiles snowdrops and crocuses to let us know that she will dance again as the light returns.

The light will always return because it is guarded by small beings and they are steadfast in their task.

Midwinter Customs

The winter solstice is the shortest day of the year, a time of darkness and cold. But it is also a time when the light slowly begins to return to the land with the promise of spring and new life. It is during this transitional period between darkness and light that we may encounter the Mari Lwyd.

This is a tradition originally from south Wales but its revival last century has seen Mari Lwyd processions rise in other places. It is usually performed between the winter solstice and Twelfth Night and to encounter one is a strange yet magnificent experience.

The Mari Lwyd (Grey Mary) consists of a horse's skull, often decorated with ribbons and other finery, which is carried on a pole by a bearer covered in a white sheet. The Mari is carried from door to door and her party attempt to gain entry into each house with a sung debate (*pwnco*) in competition with the occupants. If successful, the Mari enters the house, snapping and clacking her jaw and chasing the inhabitants before being given food and drink.

The origins of the Mari Lwyd are unclear. There are various suggestions but no records exist before the eighteenth century, yet it is certainly related to wassailing. 'Wassail' comes from the Old English *wæs hæil*, meaning 'be healthy', and relates to a number of traditions involving the sharing of food and drink and the bestowal of good health upon members of the community. This goodwill was also applied to animals and crops, in particular the apple orchards where people would go to wassail the trees.

They lit fires and sang, sometimes splashing the trees with cider. They left pieces of bread and cake, maybe as offerings to the trees but also, it is said, to attract birds such as robins which were considered lucky. Then the people would shout and bang pots and pans to frighten away disease and bad spirits that might harm the fruit harvest.

Some of these customs can still be found in the dark corners of the countryside, evolving and changing but continuing to welcome the return of the light.

Pamela Thom-Rowe

For more information on the history and customs of Wales visit: museum.wales/stfagans

Pamela Thom-Rowe's blog: myblog.moonbrookcottagehandspun.co.uk

Karin Celestine

Karin Celestine lives in a small house in Monmouth, Wales. In her garden is a shed and in the shed is another world. The world of Celestine and the Hare. It is a place where kindness, mischief and beauty help people smile.

Karin is an artist and author who creates needle felted animals of charm and character, including the stars of her own delightful stop-motion animations and her series of children's books published by Graffeg.

Her joy in the natural world is also reflected in her sculptural copper pieces which complement her feltwork.

Karin runs popular needle felting workshops, inspiring others to find their creative spirit and a membership club called the Tribe of Celestiner Chokliteers, where kindness and mischief are the order of the day.

Celestine and the Hare series

Karin has also written a series of children's books. Read about a small act of kindness in each of these nine books and learn a new craft along the way. Send us pictures of your craft to the Tribe page on Graffeg's website: www.graffeg.com.